Workaholic Bosses
Impact on Health and the Workplace

R. Dominguez Ph.D.(c)

Workaholic Bosses: Impact on Health and the Workplace

Copyright © 2024 Raul Dominguez
All rights reserved.

ISBN: 9798332083228

All rights reserved. No part of this publication may be reproduced, distributed, or transmitted in any form or by any means, including photocopying, recording, or other electronic or mechanical methods, without the prior written permission of the publisher, except in the case of brief quotations embodied in critical reviews and certain other noncommercial uses permitted by copyright law. For permission requests, write to the publisher at the address below.

Raul Dominguez, Ph.D.(c)
Miami FL, US

"To all those who tirelessly strive for success,
May you find balance amidst ambition,
And fulfillment in the journey of life.
This book is dedicated to your well-being and resilience."

INDEX

The Hidden Cost of Relentless Drive 7

Prologue 13

Chapter 1: Understanding Work Addiction 16

Chapter 2: Effects on the Boss's Health 22

Chapter 3: The Ripple Effects on Employees and Organizational Dynamics 32

Chapter 4: Strategies for Workaholic Bosses to Achieve Work-Life Balance 42

Chapter 5: Fostering a Supportive Organizational Culture 50

Chapter 6: Strategies for Achieving Work-Life Balance 56

Conclusion: Cultivating Balance and Well-being in a Workaholic World 60

References 64

The Hidden Cost of Relentless Drive

Definition of Work and Work Addiction

In today's fast-paced, competitive world, the line between dedication to one's job and addiction to work has become increasingly blurred. The term "workaholism" is often used colloquially to describe someone who works excessively and compulsively, but its implications go much deeper. According to Robinson (2000), workaholism is defined as "the compulsion or the uncontrollable need to work incessantly" (p. 2). This condition is not merely about working long hours; it's characterized by an overwhelming preoccupation with work and an inability to detach from work-related activities. Workaholism can lead to significant negative consequences for individuals, their families, and their organizations.

Understanding the difference between dedication and addiction is crucial. Dedication is driven by a passion for one's work, leading to high engagement and satisfaction. In contrast, workaholism is driven by an internal compulsion, often accompanied by anxiety, guilt, and fear of failure (Burke & Matthiesen, 2004). Dedicated workers can balance their work with personal life and other interests, while workaholics find it challenging to disconnect from work, even during personal time.

Objectives of the Book

The primary goal of this book is to shed light on the phenomenon of workaholism among bosses, exploring its origins, manifestations, and consequences. By understanding the nature of workaholism, we aim to provide insights and strategies that can help both workaholic bosses and their employees create a healthier, more productive work environment.

This book is intended for both bosses and employees. For bosses, it offers a reflective journey into understanding their work habits, the potential risks associated with them, and practical steps to mitigate these risks. For employees, it provides a framework for understanding how a workaholic boss can impact their own well-being and productivity, along with strategies to cope and thrive in such environments.

Workaholism is not merely an individual issue but a systemic one, affecting organizational culture, employee health, and overall company performance. By addressing this issue, we hope to promote healthier work environments that support both high performance and well-being.

Structure of the Book

The book is structured to provide a comprehensive understanding of workaholism and its impacts. We start by defining and understanding work addiction, followed by an exploration of its effects on the health of bosses, employees, and the organization as a whole. The latter chapters focus on practical solutions and recommendations for addressing workaholism at different levels.

Each chapter is supported by real-life examples, case studies, and credible scientific research to provide a well-rounded perspective. We draw from the works of leading psychologists and organizational researchers to ensure that our insights and recommendations are based on solid evidence.

Chapters Summary

Chapter 1: Understanding Work Addiction

This chapter introduces the concept of work addiction, examining its defining characteristics and psychological underpinnings. We explore how workaholic behaviors develop, driven by perfectionism and a relentless pursuit of success. Through real-world examples and psychological research, readers gain a comprehensive understanding of what it means to be a workaholic boss and the initial signs to watch for.

Chapter 2: Effects on the Boss's Health

Building on the foundation of work addiction, this chapter delves into the personal toll it takes on the health of workaholic bosses. We discuss the increased stress levels, risk of burnout, and physical health problems that often accompany chronic overwork. The chapter highlights the emotional and relational costs, emphasizing the importance of recognizing these impacts early.

Chapter 3: The Ripple Effects on Employees and Organizational Dynamics

Here, we explore how a boss's work addiction extends beyond personal health, affecting employees and organizational dynamics. This chapter examines the broader implications, such as decreased employee morale, higher turnover rates, and reduced innovation. We provide case studies illustrating these effects and offer insights into how workaholism can permeate and disrupt an organization.

Chapter 4: Strategies for Workaholic Bosses to Achieve Work-Life Balance

This chapter offers practical strategies for workaholic bosses to regain control over their work habits and achieve a healthier work-life balance. We present evidence-based interventions, including effective time management techniques, boundary-setting practices, and mindfulness approaches. The goal is to provide actionable steps that can lead to meaningful change in their work behavior.

Chapter 5: Fostering a Supportive Organizational Culture

Focusing on the broader organizational environment, this chapter discusses the pivotal role of culture in addressing workaholism. We explore how inclusive policies, flexible work arrangements, and well-being initiatives can create a supportive culture. Leadership's role in modeling balanced behaviors and promoting a culture of trust and resilience is also emphasized.

Chapter 6: Strategies for Achieving Work-Life Balance

In this chapter, we provide a broader perspective on work-life balance strategies applicable to all employees, not just workaholic bosses. We cover practical tools and exercises that individuals can use to assess their work habits, set realistic goals, and implement changes. This chapter is designed to empower readers to take control of their work-life balance, contributing to a healthier and more productive work environment.

The book concludes by synthesizing the key insights and strategies discussed in the previous chapters. We emphasize the importance of a holistic approach to success that integrates professional achievement with personal fulfillment. The conclusion is a call to action for leaders, employees, and organizations to prioritize well-being, foster resilience, and thrive in both their professional and personal lives

Prologue

Thriving Beyond Workaholism: Navigating Work-Life Balance in Modern Organizations

Workaholic Bosses: Impact on Health and the Workplace is a journey into the heart of one of the most pressing issues facing today's leaders and organizations: the relentless drive for success that often leads to workaholism. In this book, we will explore the complexities of workaholic behavior, its profound impact on personal well-being, and the broader implications for organizational culture.

In the opening chapters, we delve into the phenomenon of workaholism, drawing on both psychological research and real-world examples to understand its defining characteristics and consequences. You'll learn about the traits that drive workaholic bosses—such as perfectionism and an insatiable pursuit of achievement—and how these traits can lead to the sacrifice of personal health and relationships.

As we move forward, we examine the tangible effects of workaholism on individuals and organizations. Increased stress, burnout, and diminished well-being are just the beginning. We also explore how these behaviors ripple through organizations, resulting in decreased employee morale, higher turnover rates, and a stifling of creativity and innovation. Through detailed analysis and case studies, we highlight the broader implications of this pervasive issue.

Central to our discussion are practical strategies and evidence-based interventions designed to promote work-life balance. We provide actionable insights into effective time management, boundary-setting, and mindfulness practices, all tailored to help workaholic bosses and their teams achieve a healthier equilibrium. These strategies are not just theoretical; they are grounded in real-world applications that have shown tangible benefits.

Leadership and organizational culture are pivotal in shaping attitudes towards work-life balance. We will explore how inclusive policies, flexible work arrangements, and well-being initiatives can transform workplace environments. By prioritizing employee well-being, organizations can create cultures of trust, innovation, and sustainable growth. Leadership plays a crucial role in this transformation, and we offer guidance on how leaders can model and support balanced behaviors.

Throughout this book, you'll find a variety of tools designed to facilitate self-reflection and personal development. From reflection questions and actionable exercises to interactive checklists and worksheets, these resources are designed to empower you to assess your work habits, set realistic goals, and implement changes that promote balance and well-being.

In our concluding chapters, we synthesize these insights and offer a holistic approach to success that integrates professional achievement with personal fulfillment. We envision a future where workaholic bosses lead with empathy, employees thrive with resilience, and organizations flourish by prioritizing the well-being of their people.

"Workaholic Bosses: Impact on Health and the Workplace" is not just a guide; it's a call to action for leaders, employees, and organizations to embrace a balanced and fulfilling approach to work and life. As you read through these pages, we hope you find the inspiration and tools you need to navigate the complexities of modern work environments and achieve a sustainable, thriving future.

Welcome to the journey towards thriving beyond workaholism. Let's begin.

Chapter 1: Understanding Work Addiction

Characteristics of a Workaholic Boss

Workaholic bosses are often perceived as the backbone of any organization due to their relentless dedication and seemingly boundless energy. However, beneath the surface lies a complex and potentially destructive pattern of behavior. Understanding these characteristics is crucial for identifying and addressing work addiction.

Obsessive Need to Control: Workaholic bosses often exhibit an obsessive need to control every aspect of their work environment. This control manifests in micromanagement, reluctance to delegate tasks, and a tendency to involve themselves in minute details that could be handled by others. Such behavior stems from a deep-seated fear of failure and a belief that their direct involvement is the only way to ensure success (Porter, 2001).

Inability to Disconnect: One defining trait of a workaholic boss is the inability to disconnect from work. Whether it's checking emails late at night, working through weekends, or constantly thinking about work even during personal time, this inability to disengage from work-related activities is a hallmark of work addiction (Robinson, 2000). This behavior not only affects the boss but sets a precedent for the entire organization, creating a culture where constant availability is expected.

Excessive Hours and Unreasonable Expectations: Workaholic bosses often work excessive hours and have high expectations for themselves and their employees. They may arrive early, leave late, and often expect their team to follow suit. These unreasonable expectations can lead to a toxic work environment where employees feel pressured to sacrifice their personal time to meet the boss's standards (Burke & Matthiesen, 2004).

Perfectionism: Perfectionism is another characteristic commonly observed in workaholic bosses. They set exceptionally high standards for themselves and others, often to the point of being unrealistic. This perfectionism can lead to a cycle of overwork, as the boss continuously strives for flawless outcomes, sometimes at the expense of efficiency and practicality (Stoeber & Damian, 2016).

Emotional Detachment: Despite their intense involvement in work, workaholic bosses often exhibit emotional detachment from their colleagues and subordinates. They may seem unapproachable, unsympathetic, or indifferent to the personal needs and challenges of their team. This detachment can create a sense of isolation among employees, leading to decreased morale and engagement (Ng, Sorensen, & Feldman, 2007).

Lack of Work-Life Balance: The imbalance between professional and personal life is a critical indicator of work addiction. Workaholic bosses often neglect their personal lives, including relationships, hobbies, and self-care activities. This lack of balance not only affects their well-being but also sends a message to employees that work should always come first, perpetuating a culture of overwork (Taris, Schaufeli, & Verhoeven, 2005).

Real-Life Examples and Case Studies

Case Study: Sarah, the Tireless Executive: Sarah was known as the tireless executive who could always be found at her desk, no matter the hour. Her dedication was legendary, and she was often praised for her hard work and commitment. However, Sarah's work habits soon began to take a toll on her health and personal life. She suffered from chronic stress, insomnia, and a strained relationship with her family. Her team, inspired but also intimidated by her work ethic, started to experience burnout and dissatisfaction. Sarah's story highlights how work addiction can start as a commendable trait but quickly turn into a detrimental pattern that affects both the individual and the organization.

Example: The High-Performing Startup: In a high-performing startup, the CEO, John, was celebrated for his relentless pursuit of success. He worked long hours and expected his team to match his pace. Initially, the company thrived, fueled by John's energy and drive. However, over time, the constant pressure led to high turnover rates, with many employees citing burnout and lack of work-life balance as their reasons for leaving. The company's culture of overwork, driven by John's workaholism, ultimately hindered its growth and sustainability.

Causes of Work Addiction

Psychological Factors: Several psychological factors contribute to work addiction. One major factor is the need for control. Workaholic bosses often have a strong desire to control outcomes and processes, which can stem from perfectionism and fear of failure. This need for control drives them to micromanage and overwork, believing that their direct involvement is crucial for success (Porter, 2001).

Another psychological factor is self-worth. Many workaholic bosses tie their self-esteem and identity to their professional achievements. They believe that their value as individuals is directly linked to their productivity and success at work. This belief system pushes them to work excessively, often at the expense of their personal lives and health (Ng, Sorensen, & Feldman, 2007).

Social and Cultural Factors: Social and cultural factors also play a significant role in fostering work addiction. In many societies, there is a cultural norm that equates long hours with dedication and success. This norm is often reinforced by organizational cultures that reward overwork and penalize perceived underperformance. In such environments, workaholic behavior is not only accepted but encouraged, leading to a cycle of overwork and burnout (Burke & Matthiesen, 2004).

Moreover, the rise of technology has blurred the boundaries between work and personal life. With smartphones and laptops, employees are always connected, making it difficult to disconnect from work.

This constant connectivity can exacerbate workaholic tendencies, as bosses and employees alike feel the pressure to be available and responsive at all times (Robinson, 2000).

Relevant Psychological Definitions

Burnout: Burnout is a state of chronic physical and emotional exhaustion caused by prolonged exposure to stress and overwork. It is characterized by feelings of fatigue, cynicism, and a sense of reduced professional efficacy. Burnout can result from workaholism, as the constant pressure to perform and the inability to disconnect from work lead to depletion of energy and motivation (Maslach, Schaufeli, & Leiter, 2001).

Workaholism: Workaholism, or work addiction, is the compulsion to work excessively and compulsively, often at the expense of personal health and relationships. Unlike dedicated workers who find joy and fulfillment in their work, workaholics are driven by an internal need to work, accompanied by feelings of guilt and anxiety when not working. This compulsive behavior can lead to negative outcomes for both the individual and the organization (Robinson, 2000).

Work-Life Balance: Work-life balance refers to the ability to maintain a healthy equilibrium between work responsibilities and personal life. Achieving work-life balance involves setting boundaries, prioritizing self-care, and ensuring that work does not encroach on personal time. For workaholic bosses, achieving work-life balance is particularly challenging, as their compulsive work habits often overshadow other aspects of their lives (Taris, Schaufeli, & Verhoeven, 2005).

Understanding the characteristics and causes of work addiction is the first step in addressing this pervasive issue. Workaholic bosses exhibit behaviors that not only affect their health and well-being but also have far-reaching consequences for their employees and organizations. By recognizing these traits and understanding the underlying psychological and social factors, we can begin to develop strategies to mitigate the impact of work addiction and promote healthier work environments.

The following chapters will delve deeper into the specific effects of work addiction on the health of bosses, employees, and organizations, providing a comprehensive view of this complex issue. Through real-life examples, case studies, and scientific research, we aim to offer insights and practical solutions that can help create a more balanced and productive workplace.

Chapter 2: Effects on the Boss's Health

Impact on Mental Health

Workaholic bosses are often perceived as highly driven and successful individuals. However, the relentless pursuit of work often comes at a significant cost to their mental health. The impact of work addiction on mental health is profound and multifaceted, encompassing chronic stress, anxiety, depression, and a range of other psychological issues.

Chronic Stress: One of the most immediate and pervasive effects of workaholism is chronic stress. Unlike acute stress, which is temporary and can sometimes be beneficial, chronic stress persists over long periods and has detrimental effects on mental and physical health. Workaholic bosses are in a constant state of high alert, driven by the incessant need to meet their own high standards and expectations. This continuous pressure activates the body's stress response system, leading to elevated levels of cortisol and other stress hormones (Selye, 1976).

Over time, chronic stress can lead to burnout, a state of emotional, physical, and mental exhaustion caused by prolonged and excessive stress (Maslach, Schaufeli, & Leiter, 2001). Burnout is characterized by feelings of cynicism, detachment from work, and a sense of ineffectiveness and lack of accomplishment. For workaholic bosses, burnout can severely impair their ability to function effectively, both professionally and personally.

Anxiety and Depression: The constant pressure to perform and the inability to disconnect from work can also lead to significant anxiety and depression. Workaholic bosses often experience high levels of anxiety related to their work performance and the fear of failure. This anxiety can manifest in various ways, including restlessness, difficulty concentrating, irritability, and sleep disturbances (American Psychiatric Association, 2013).

Depression is another common consequence of workaholism. The relentless pursuit of work at the expense of personal and social activities can lead to feelings of isolation, hopelessness, and sadness. Research indicates that individuals who work excessively and compulsively are at a higher risk of developing depressive symptoms (Shimazu et al., 2012). Depression not only affects the individual's well-being but also their professional performance and relationships with colleagues and family.

Micromanaging and Its Psychological Impact: Micromanaging, a common trait among workaholic bosses, exacerbates these mental health issues. Micromanagement involves excessively controlling and scrutinizing employees' work, often driven by a need for perfection and fear of delegation (Porter, 2001). This behavior stems from the workaholic's deep-seated need for control and their inability to trust others to meet their high standards.

Micromanaging increases the workaholic boss's workload, as they take on tasks that should be delegated. This added burden heightens stress and anxiety, creating a vicious cycle. Moreover, the constant vigilance required to micromanage leads to mental fatigue and cognitive overload, further impairing their mental health (Hülsheger et al., 2014).

Impact on Physical Health

The toll of work addiction is not limited to mental health; it extends to physical health as well. The excessive hours, chronic stress, and unhealthy work habits associated with workaholism can lead to a range of physical health problems.

Cardiovascular Diseases: One of the most serious physical health risks associated with workaholism is cardiovascular disease. Chronic stress and long working hours are significant risk factors for heart disease, hypertension, and stroke. Studies have shown that individuals who work excessively long hours have a higher risk of developing cardiovascular conditions due to the constant activation of the body's stress response and unhealthy lifestyle choices, such as poor diet and lack of exercise (Kivimäki et al., 2015).

Gastrointestinal Issues: Workaholic bosses often neglect their dietary needs, opting for quick, unhealthy meals or skipping meals altogether. This neglect can lead to gastrointestinal problems such as ulcers, irritable bowel syndrome (IBS), and other digestive disorders. The gut-brain axis, which links the emotional and cognitive centers of the brain with peripheral intestinal functions, plays a critical role in this connection. Chronic stress can disrupt this axis, leading to various gastrointestinal issues (Mayer, 2011).

Sleep Problems: Sleep is essential for physical health, and its deprivation can have severe consequences. Workaholic bosses often sacrifice sleep to meet their work demands, leading to chronic sleep deprivation. Lack of sleep affects cognitive function, emotional regulation, and overall health. It increases the risk of various health problems, including obesity, diabetes, cardiovascular disease, and impaired immune function (Walker, 2017). Furthermore, the anxiety and stress associated with workaholism can lead to insomnia, creating a cycle of poor sleep and deteriorating health.

Chronic Fatigue: The relentless pace at which workaholic bosses operate often leads to chronic fatigue. This condition is characterized by persistent and overwhelming tiredness that is not relieved by rest or sleep. Chronic fatigue can significantly impair cognitive function, decision-making abilities, and physical health. It reduces the individual's capacity to cope with stress and increases the risk of accidents and errors (Sharpe & Wilks, 2002).

Impact on Sexual Life and Relationships

The detrimental effects of workaholism extend beyond professional and personal health, significantly impacting the sexual life and relationships of workaholic bosses. The constant pressure to perform, long working hours, and chronic stress associated with work addiction can create substantial barriers to maintaining healthy and fulfilling intimate relationships.

Decreased Libido and Sexual Dysfunction: Chronic stress, a hallmark of workaholism, has a direct impact on sexual health. Elevated levels of stress hormones like cortisol can reduce libido and lead to sexual dysfunction in both men and women. Stress can interfere with the body's natural sexual response, leading to difficulties such as erectile dysfunction in men and reduced sexual arousal and satisfaction in women (Charnetski & Brennan, 2001).

Moreover, the physical and mental exhaustion resulting from long working hours can diminish sexual desire and energy. Workaholic bosses often prioritize work over their personal lives, leaving little time or energy for sexual intimacy. This neglect can strain relationships and lead to dissatisfaction and frustration for both partners (Rosen, 2000).

Relationship Strain: Workaholism also places significant strain on relationships. The relentless focus on work often leads to neglect of personal and family time. Partners of workaholic bosses may feel ignored, undervalued, and disconnected, leading to resentment and conflict. The lack of emotional and physical intimacy can erode the foundation of the relationship, resulting in increased tension and a higher likelihood of separation or divorce (Robinson, 2000).

The tendency to micromanage can extend into personal relationships, creating additional friction. Workaholic bosses may exhibit controlling behaviors at home, mirroring their work habits. This can lead to power struggles and communication breakdowns, further damaging the relationship (Porter, 2001).

Emotional Distance: The emotional detachment associated with burnout and chronic stress can create a barrier to intimacy. Workaholic bosses may become emotionally distant and less responsive to their partner's needs. This detachment can make it difficult for them to connect on an emotional level, leading to feelings of loneliness and isolation for both partners (Maslach, Schaufeli, & Leiter, 2001).

Additionally, the perfectionism often associated with workaholism can translate into unrealistic expectations in personal relationships. The workaholic boss may demand the same level of perfection and commitment from their partner, leading to constant dissatisfaction and conflict (Stoeber & Damian, 2016).

Impact on Family Life: The effects of workaholism extend to family life as well. Children of workaholic bosses may feel neglected and lack emotional support, leading to behavioral and emotional issues. The absence of a parent due to excessive work can affect a child's sense of security and well-being, leading to long-term psychological consequences (Robinson, 2000).

Workaholic bosses may also miss out on important family events and milestones, further straining familial bonds. The inability to balance work and family responsibilities can lead to feelings of guilt and inadequacy, contributing to the overall stress and mental health issues faced by the workaholic boss (Ng, Sorensen, & Feldman, 2007).

Relevant Studies and Data

Research has highlighted the significant impact of workaholism on sexual life and relationships. A study by Burke and Matthiesen (2004) found that workaholic managers reported lower levels of marital satisfaction and higher levels of family conflict compared to their non-workaholic counterparts. The study also indicated that workaholism was associated with lower levels of sexual satisfaction and intimacy.

Another study by Taris, Schaufeli, and Verhoeven (2005) examined the effects of workaholism on relationship quality. The findings indicated that workaholism was negatively related to relationship quality, with workaholic individuals reporting higher levels of relationship conflict and lower levels of relationship satisfaction.

Practical Implications

Addressing the impact of workaholism on sexual life and relationships requires a comprehensive approach that includes both individual and organizational strategies. Here are some practical implications and recommendations:

Promoting Work-Life Balance: Encouraging a healthy work-life balance is crucial for maintaining healthy relationships. Organizations should promote policies that support work-life balance, such as flexible working hours, remote work options, and adequate vacation time. These measures can help workaholic bosses spend more quality time with their partners and families, strengthening their relationships (Kossek, Baltes, & Matthews, 2011).

Providing Relationship Counseling: Access to relationship counseling and support services can help workaholic bosses and their partners address the challenges posed by work addiction. Counseling can provide a safe space for partners to communicate their needs and concerns, improve their understanding of each other, and develop strategies to enhance their relationship (Gottman & Silver, 1999).

Encouraging Mindfulness and Stress Reduction Techniques: Incorporating mindfulness and stress reduction techniques can help workaholic bosses manage their stress levels and improve their emotional well-being. Practices such as meditation, deep breathing exercises, and yoga can reduce stress, enhance emotional regulation, and promote a greater sense of presence in personal relationships (Kabat-Zinn, 1990). These techniques can help workaholic bosses become more attuned to their partner's needs and foster deeper emotional connections.

Promoting Healthy Communication: Healthy communication is essential for maintaining strong relationships. Organizations can offer training programs that focus on effective communication skills, conflict resolution, and emotional intelligence. These skills can help workaholic bosses communicate more effectively with their partners, express their feelings and needs, and resolve conflicts in a constructive manner (Goleman, 1995).

Setting Boundaries and Prioritizing Relationships: Workaholic bosses need to set clear boundaries between work and personal life. This includes establishing designated work hours, limiting work-related communication outside of those hours, and prioritizing time with their partners and families. By consciously allocating time for personal relationships, workaholic bosses can strengthen their emotional bonds and enhance their overall well-being (Perlow, 1999).

Engaging in Shared Activities: Participating in shared activities and hobbies can strengthen the bond between workaholic bosses and their partners. Engaging in activities that both partners enjoy can foster a sense of connection and create positive shared experiences. These activities can range from simple daily routines, such as cooking together, to more elaborate plans like weekend getaways or vacations (Aron, Norman, Aron, & Lewandowski, 2002).

The impact of workaholism on sexual life and relationships is profound and far-reaching. Chronic stress, decreased libido, emotional distance, and relationship strain are just some of the consequences faced by workaholic bosses. The tendency to micromanage, neglect personal time, and prioritize work over relationships exacerbates these issues, leading to dissatisfaction and conflict in intimate relationships.

Addressing the negative effects of workaholism on relationships requires a multifaceted approach. Promoting work-life balance, providing access to relationship counseling, encouraging mindfulness and stress reduction techniques, fostering healthy communication, setting boundaries, and engaging in shared activities are essential strategies to mitigate the impact of workaholism on relationships.

By understanding and addressing the challenges posed by work addiction, workaholic bosses can improve their personal relationships and overall well-being. The next chapter will explore the effects of workaholism on employees and organizational dynamics, providing further insights into the pervasive impact of this issue and offering practical solutions to create healthier and more balanced work environments.

Chapter 3: The Ripple Effects on Employees and Organizational Dynamics

The Immediate Impact on Employees

The behaviors and attitudes of workaholic bosses extend far beyond their personal lives and have significant repercussions for their employees. These effects can manifest in various ways, including increased stress levels, decreased job satisfaction, and a pervasive sense of insecurity among the workforce.

Increased Stress Levels: Employees working under workaholic bosses often experience elevated stress levels. These bosses tend to impose their own high standards and expectations on their subordinates, leading to unrealistic workloads and pressure to perform at exceptional levels consistently. This heightened stress is a direct result of the micromanagement and constant oversight typical of workaholic leaders. Studies have shown that excessive managerial control and lack of autonomy at work are strongly correlated with increased employee stress and burnout (Karasek, 1979; Bakker et al., 2005).

Moreover, workaholic bosses frequently blur the boundaries between work and personal life for their employees, expecting them to be available outside of regular working hours and during weekends. This lack of work-life balance significantly contributes to chronic stress, as employees feel perpetually on call and unable to fully disengage from work-related demands (Boswell & Olson-Buchanan, 2007).

Decreased Job Satisfaction: The high demands and relentless pace set by workaholic bosses often lead to decreased job satisfaction among employees. When employees are consistently pushed to their limits without adequate recognition or reward, their motivation and engagement levels diminish. Research indicates that job satisfaction is closely linked to perceptions of fairness, recognition, and support from management (Judge et al., 2001).

Workaholic bosses, with their focus on results and productivity, may overlook the importance of positive reinforcement and support for their employees. This lack of recognition can make employees feel undervalued and unappreciated, further decreasing their job satisfaction. Additionally, the constant pressure to meet high expectations can lead to a toxic work environment, characterized by fear, competition, and a lack of collaboration (Rhoades & Eisenberger, 2002).

Insecurity and Job Anxiety: Workaholic bosses often create an atmosphere of insecurity and job anxiety. Their perfectionist tendencies and high expectations can make employees feel that their job security is constantly at risk. The fear of not meeting these expectations or making mistakes can lead to significant job anxiety, negatively impacting employee performance and well-being (Ashford, Lee, & Bobko, 1989).

Furthermore, workaholic bosses may exhibit unpredictable behavior, such as sudden changes in priorities or expectations. This unpredictability creates an unstable work environment where employees are unsure of what is expected of them, leading to increased anxiety and decreased confidence in their roles (Katz & Kahn, 1978).

The Long-Term Consequences for Employees

The long-term consequences of working under a workaholic boss can be even more severe, affecting employees' mental and physical health, career development, and overall quality of life.

Mental Health Issues: Prolonged exposure to high stress and job insecurity can lead to serious mental health issues for employees. Chronic stress is a major risk factor for conditions such as anxiety disorders, depression, and burnout. Employees working under constant pressure may develop symptoms of these conditions, including persistent feelings of worry, sadness, fatigue, and loss of interest in work and other activities (Melchior et al., 2007).

Burnout, in particular, is a significant concern in high-pressure work environments. It is characterized by emotional exhaustion, depersonalization, and a reduced sense of personal accomplishment. Burnout not only affects an employee's performance but also their overall quality of life and mental health (Maslach & Jackson, 1981). The prevalence of burnout in workplaces led by workaholic bosses underscores the need for organizational interventions to address and mitigate these issues.

Physical Health Problems: The physical health of employees can also be adversely affected by the stress and demands of working under a workaholic boss. Chronic stress is linked to a range of physical health problems, including cardiovascular disease, gastrointestinal issues, and weakened immune function (Sapolsky, 2004). Employees experiencing high levels of stress may also engage in unhealthy coping mechanisms, such as poor dietary habits, lack of exercise, and substance abuse, further exacerbating their health problems (Aldana & Pronk, 2001).

Career Development and Job Satisfaction: Workaholic bosses can hinder the career development and job satisfaction of their employees. The high demands and pressure can create an environment where employees are more focused on immediate survival rather than long-term growth and development. Opportunities for skill development, creativity, and career advancement may be limited as employees are constantly striving to meet the high expectations set by their boss (Hobfoll, 1989).

Additionally, the lack of recognition and support from workaholic bosses can lead to decreased motivation and engagement. Employees who feel undervalued and unsupported are less likely to be committed to their organization and may seek opportunities elsewhere, leading to higher turnover rates and loss of talent for the company (Meyer & Allen, 1991).

The Organizational Impact

The effects of workaholic bosses are not confined to individual employees; they ripple out to impact the entire organization. The organizational culture, productivity, and overall success of the company can be significantly influenced by the presence of workaholic leadership.

Negative Organizational Culture: Workaholic bosses often create a negative organizational culture characterized by high pressure, competition, and fear of failure. This type of culture can be detrimental to employee morale and engagement. When the organizational focus is solely on productivity and results, employees may feel dehumanized and undervalued. This can lead to a lack of trust, collaboration, and open communication within the team (Schein, 2010).

Moreover, a culture driven by workaholism can perpetuate unhealthy work habits among employees. Seeing their boss constantly working long hours and neglecting personal time may set an implicit expectation that they should do the same. This can lead to widespread burnout and decreased overall well-being within the organization (Porter, 2001).

Decreased Productivity and Innovation: While workaholic bosses may drive short-term productivity through high demands and constant pressure, the long-term impact on productivity can be negative. Chronic stress and burnout among employees can lead to decreased efficiency, higher error rates, and reduced creativity. Employees who are exhausted and overwhelmed are less likely to engage in innovative thinking and problem-solving (Amabile et al., 1996).

Furthermore, high turnover rates resulting from employee dissatisfaction and burnout can disrupt organizational continuity and productivity. The constant need to recruit and train new employees can drain organizational resources and hinder long-term success (Huselid, 1995).

Financial Costs: The financial costs associated with workaholic leadership are significant. Increased healthcare costs due to stress-related illnesses, higher turnover rates, and decreased productivity all contribute to the financial burden on the organization. Investing in employee well-being and creating a supportive work environment can mitigate these costs and promote long-term organizational health (Goetzel et al., 2002).

Strategies for Mitigating the Negative Impact

Addressing the negative impact of workaholic bosses on employees and organizational dynamics requires a comprehensive approach that involves both individual and organizational strategies.

Promoting Work-Life Balance: Organizations should promote a culture of work-life balance by implementing policies and practices that support employees' well-being. This includes flexible working hours, remote work options, and encouraging employees to take regular breaks and vacations. By prioritizing work-life balance, organizations can reduce employee stress and burnout and promote a healthier, more productive workforce (Kossek et al., 2011).

Providing Training and Support for Leaders: Training and support for leaders are crucial in addressing workaholism at the managerial level. Leadership development programs should focus on emotional intelligence, stress management, and effective communication skills. Providing workaholic bosses with the tools and resources to manage their stress and adopt healthier work habits can lead to a more supportive and balanced work environment (Goleman, 1995).

Encouraging Open Communication: Creating an environment of open communication where employees feel safe to express their concerns and needs is essential. Regular feedback sessions, anonymous surveys, and open-door policies can help identify issues related to workaholism and allow for timely interventions. Encouraging a culture of transparency and trust can improve employee morale and engagement (Detert & Burris, 2007).

Implementing Employee Well-Being Programs: Organizations should implement comprehensive employee well-being programs that address both physical and mental health. These programs can include stress management workshops, access to mental health resources, fitness programs, and initiatives that promote healthy lifestyle choices. Supporting employees' overall well-being can enhance their resilience and productivity (Richardson & Rothstein, 2008).

Setting Realistic Expectations: Leaders should set realistic expectations for their employees, recognizing the importance of work-life balance and sustainable productivity. Clear communication of goals, deadlines, and performance standards can help employees manage their workloads effectively without feeling overwhelmed. Encouraging employees to set boundaries and prioritize their well-being can lead to a healthier and more productive work environment (Hackman & Oldham, 1976).

Case Studies and Real-World Examples

Several organizations have successfully implemented strategies to address the negative impact of workaholism and promote a healthier work environment.

Google's Approach to Work-Life Balance: Google is known for its innovative approach to employee well-being and work-life balance. The company offers a range of benefits, including flexible work hours, on-site wellness programs, and generous parental leave policies. Google also promotes a culture of open communication and transparency, encouraging employees to provide feedback and voice their concerns. These initiatives have contributed to high levels of employee satisfaction and engagement, demonstrating the positive impact of prioritizing work-life balance (Schmidt & Rosenberg, 2014).

Deloitte's Focus on Mental Health: Deloitte has implemented a comprehensive mental health program to support its employees' well-being. The program includes mental health awareness training for managers, access to counseling services, and initiatives to reduce the stigma associated with mental health issues. Deloitte also encourages work-life balance through flexible working arrangements and promotes a supportive organizational culture. These efforts have resulted in a more engaged and productive workforce, showcasing the benefits of addressing mental health in the workplace (Deloitte, 2020).

Salesforce's Commitment to Employee Wellness: Salesforce has made a strong commitment to employee wellness by offering various wellness programs and resources. The company provides on-site fitness centers, wellness coaching, and mindfulness training to help employees manage stress and maintain a healthy work-life balance. Salesforce also emphasizes the importance of mental health, offering comprehensive mental health benefits and promoting a culture of support and understanding. These initiatives have helped create a positive work environment where employees feel valued and supported (Salesforce, 2021).

Unilever's Holistic Approach to Well-Being: Unilever has adopted a holistic approach to employee well-being, recognizing the interconnectedness of physical, mental, and emotional health. The company offers a range of wellness programs, including stress management workshops, healthy eating initiatives, and fitness challenges. Unilever also prioritizes work-life balance through flexible work arrangements and encourages employees to take regular breaks and vacations. This comprehensive approach has led to improved employee satisfaction and reduced turnover rates (Unilever, 2019).

The impact of workaholic bosses on employees and organizational dynamics is profound and multifaceted. The immediate effects, such as increased stress levels, decreased job satisfaction, and job anxiety, can significantly harm employees' mental and physical health. In the long term, these effects can lead to serious mental health issues, physical health problems, and hindered career development.

For the organization, the presence of workaholic leadership can create a negative organizational culture, decrease productivity and innovation, and incur substantial financial costs. Addressing these issues requires a comprehensive approach that includes promoting work-life balance, providing training and support for leaders, encouraging open communication, implementing employee well-being programs, and setting realistic expectations.

Real-world examples from companies like Google, Deloitte, Salesforce, and Unilever demonstrate the effectiveness of these strategies in creating a healthier and more productive work environment. By prioritizing the well-being of employees and fostering a supportive organizational culture, companies can mitigate the negative impact of workaholic bosses and promote long-term success.

Chapter 4: Strategies for Workaholic Bosses to Achieve Work-Life Balance

Understanding the Workaholic Mentality

To develop effective strategies for workaholic bosses to achieve work-life balance, it's crucial first to understand the mentality driving their behavior. Workaholism, unlike dedication or hard work, is often rooted in deeper psychological issues such as the need for control, fear of failure, or a compulsion to achieve and prove one's worth (Oates, 1971).

The Role of Perfectionism: Many workaholic bosses exhibit perfectionist tendencies, where they set excessively high standards for themselves and others. This perfectionism can lead to constant dissatisfaction with their own and their employees' performance, perpetuating a cycle of overwork and stress. Research indicates that perfectionism is a significant predictor of workaholism, contributing to both psychological and physical strain (Stoeber & Damian, 2016).

Fear of Failure: Another common trait among workaholic bosses is an intense fear of failure. This fear drives them to put in excessive hours and maintain a relentless pace to avoid any possibility of falling short. The psychological toll of this fear can be profound, leading to anxiety and a diminished sense of personal well-being (Spence & Robbins, 1992).

Need for Control: Workaholic bosses often feel a strong need to control every aspect of their work environment. This need for control can manifest in micromanagement, where they closely monitor and direct their employees' work. Micromanagement not only increases their own stress but also stifles employee autonomy and creativity, creating a toxic work environment (Deci & Ryan, 1987).

Strategies for Achieving Work-Life Balance

Workaholic bosses can implement various strategies to achieve a healthier work-life balance, which can lead to improved well-being for themselves and their employees.

1. Self-Reflection and Awareness: The first step towards change is self-awareness. Workaholic bosses must recognize and acknowledge their behavior patterns and the underlying motivations driving their workaholism. This self-reflection can be facilitated through journaling, mindfulness practices, or working with a coach or therapist specializing in work-related issues (Kabat-Zinn, 1994).

2. Setting Realistic Goals and Boundaries: Workaholic bosses should practice setting realistic goals and boundaries. This involves prioritizing tasks based on importance and urgency, delegating responsibilities, and learning to say no to additional commitments that may lead to overwork. Setting clear boundaries between work and personal life, such as not checking emails after hours or during weekends, can help create a healthier balance (Covey, 1989).

3. Developing Time Management Skills: Effective time management is crucial for reducing workaholic tendencies. Workaholic bosses can benefit from techniques such as time blocking, where specific times are allocated for focused work, meetings, and personal activities. Tools like calendars, to-do lists, and productivity apps can also help manage time more efficiently and prevent work from spilling into personal time (Allen, 2001).

4. Prioritizing Health and Well-Being: Maintaining physical and mental health is essential for achieving work-life balance. Workaholic bosses should prioritize regular exercise, a healthy diet, and sufficient sleep. Incorporating stress-reducing activities such as meditation, yoga, or hobbies can also improve overall well-being. Encouraging these practices within the workplace can create a culture that values health and balance (Siegrist, 1996).

5. Encouraging Open Communication and Feedback: Creating an environment where employees feel comfortable providing feedback can help workaholic bosses understand the impact of their behavior. Regular check-ins, anonymous surveys, and open-door policies can facilitate honest communication. By listening to their employees' concerns, workaholic bosses can make necessary adjustments to their leadership style and work habits (Detert & Burris, 2007).

6. Delegating and Empowering Employees: Delegation is a critical skill for reducing workload and empowering employees. Workaholic bosses should identify tasks that can be delegated and trust their team members to handle them. Empowering employees with autonomy and decision-making authority not only reduces the boss's workload but also fosters a sense of ownership and engagement among employees (Hackman & Oldham, 1976).

7. Seeking Professional Help: In some cases, workaholic bosses may need professional help to address underlying psychological issues. Therapy or coaching can provide tools and strategies to manage workaholic tendencies and develop healthier work habits. Cognitive-behavioral therapy (CBT), for instance, can help individuals reframe negative thought patterns and behaviors related to work (Beck, 2011).

Implementing Organizational Support Systems

Organizations play a vital role in supporting workaholic bosses and promoting a healthy work-life balance. By implementing supportive policies and practices, companies can create an environment conducive to balance and well-being.

1. Promoting a Balanced Work Culture: Organizations should actively promote a culture that values work-life balance. This can be achieved through leadership training, communication campaigns, and recognition programs that celebrate employees who demonstrate a healthy balance between work and personal life. A balanced work culture encourages employees to take breaks, use their vacation time, and prioritize their well-being (Kossek et al., 2011).

2. Offering Flexible Work Arrangements: Flexible work arrangements, such as remote work, flexible hours, and compressed workweeks, can help workaholic bosses and their employees achieve better work-life balance. These arrangements provide individuals with greater control over their schedules, allowing them to manage work alongside personal responsibilities more effectively (Golden, 2001).

3. Providing Access to Mental Health Resources: Access to mental health resources is essential for supporting workaholic bosses and employees. Organizations should offer comprehensive mental health benefits, including counseling services, stress management programs, and wellness initiatives. Promoting mental health awareness and reducing stigma associated with seeking help can encourage individuals to utilize these resources (Richardson & Rothstein, 2008).

4. Encouraging Regular Breaks and Time Off: Encouraging employees, including workaholic bosses, to take regular breaks and time off is crucial for preventing burnout. Organizations should promote policies that support taking vacations, personal days, and regular breaks during the workday. Managers can lead by example by taking their own time off and respecting their employees' need for rest (Fritz & Sonnentag, 2006).

5. Implementing Wellness Programs: Comprehensive wellness programs that address physical, mental, and emotional health can significantly benefit workaholic bosses and employees. These programs can include fitness challenges, nutrition workshops, stress management sessions, and mindfulness training. By investing in employee well-being, organizations can create a healthier, more productive workforce (Goetzel et al., 2002).

6. Fostering Open Dialogue About Workaholism: Creating an open dialogue about workaholism within the organization can help destigmatize the issue and encourage individuals to seek support. Workshops, seminars, and discussions on the topic can raise awareness and provide strategies for managing workaholic tendencies. Encouraging leaders to share their experiences and challenges can also promote a culture of transparency and support (Schein, 2010).

Case Studies and Best Practices

Several organizations have successfully implemented strategies to support workaholic bosses and promote work-life balance, providing valuable insights and best practices.

Ernst & Young's Flexible Work Policy: Ernst & Young (EY) has implemented a flexible work policy that allows employees to choose their working hours and locations. This policy supports work-life balance and reduces the pressure to conform to traditional work schedules. EY also offers wellness programs and mental health resources, demonstrating a commitment to employee well-being. These initiatives have contributed to higher employee satisfaction and retention rates (EY, 2019).

Microsoft's Emphasis on Employee Well-Being: Microsoft has prioritized employee well-being through various initiatives, including flexible work arrangements, mental health support, and wellness programs. The company encourages a balanced work culture by promoting regular breaks, vacation time, and work-life balance workshops. Microsoft's focus on well-being has led to increased employee engagement and productivity (Microsoft, 2020).

Adobe's Approach to Work-Life Balance: Adobe has implemented several strategies to support work-life balance, including flexible work schedules, wellness programs, and mental health resources. The company promotes a culture of open communication and encourages employees to prioritize their well-being. Adobe's commitment to work-life balance has resulted in a positive work environment and high levels of employee satisfaction (Adobe, 2018).

American Express' Comprehensive Wellness Programs: American Express offers comprehensive wellness programs that address physical, mental, and emotional health. These programs include fitness challenges, stress management workshops, and access to mental health resources. The company also promotes work-life balance through flexible work arrangements and encourages employees to take regular breaks and time off. American Express' focus on well-being has led to a healthier, more engaged workforce (American Express, 2017).

Achieving work-life balance is a complex but essential goal for workaholic bosses. By understanding the underlying motivations driving their behavior and implementing effective strategies, they can improve their well-being and create a more positive work environment for their employees. Organizations play a crucial role in supporting workaholic bosses by promoting a balanced work culture, offering flexible work arrangements, providing access to mental health resources, and encouraging regular breaks and time off.

Real-world examples from companies like Ernst & Young, Microsoft, Adobe, and American Express demonstrate the effectiveness of these strategies in fostering a healthy work-life balance. By prioritizing employee well-being and creating a supportive organizational culture, companies can mitigate the negative impact of workaholism and promote long-term success.

Chapter 5: Fostering a Supportive Organizational Culture

Organizational culture is the bedrock upon which attitudes, behaviors, and norms are built within a workplace. It encompasses the shared values, beliefs, and practices that shape the overall environment and employee experience (Schein, 2010). For workaholic bosses aiming to achieve work-life balance, creating a supportive organizational culture is crucial. Such a culture not only benefits individual well-being but also contributes to organizational success by fostering engagement, productivity, and retention (Kossek et al., 2011).

The Importance of Organizational Culture in Work-Life Balance: A positive organizational culture that prioritizes work-life balance can mitigate stress, reduce burnout, and enhance overall job satisfaction among employees (Golden, 2001). Research indicates that organizations with supportive cultures experience higher levels of employee commitment and performance, as employees feel valued and supported in managing their personal and professional lives effectively (Detert & Burris, 2007).

Key Elements of a Supportive Organizational Culture:

1. **Leadership Commitment:** Leadership sets the tone for organizational culture. When leaders prioritize and model work-life balance behaviors, it signals to employees, including workaholic bosses, that balance is valued. Leaders who demonstrate flexibility, respect for personal time, and encourage healthy boundaries contribute significantly to a positive work environment (Goleman, 1995).

2. **Transparent Policies and Practices:** Clear and consistent policies related to flexible work arrangements, telecommuting options, leave policies, and expectations around work hours are essential. Transparent communication ensures that employees understand their rights and responsibilities, fostering trust and reducing ambiguity (Fritz & Sonnentag, 2006).

3. **Supportive Resources:** Providing resources such as employee assistance programs, wellness initiatives, mental health support, and access to financial planning can help employees navigate personal challenges effectively. These resources demonstrate organizational commitment to employee well-being and resilience (Johnson & Johnson, 2018).

4. **Open Communication and Feedback:** Establishing open channels for communication and feedback allows employees to voice concerns, share ideas, and seek support. Regular

check-ins, employee surveys, and town hall meetings provide opportunities for dialogue around work-life balance issues and organizational culture (Deci & Ryan, 1987).

Strategies for Fostering Work-Life Balance

Implementing effective strategies to foster work-life balance requires a comprehensive approach that addresses cultural, structural, and individual factors within the organization.

1. Leadership Development Programs: Investing in leadership development programs that emphasize work-life balance can empower leaders to create supportive environments. These programs should educate leaders on effective time management, delegation skills, and the importance of setting realistic expectations. Leadership development also includes training on recognizing signs of burnout and promoting resilience (Hackman & Oldham, 1976).

2. Cultural Sensitivity and Inclusivity Training: Cultural sensitivity training promotes awareness and understanding of diverse perspectives related to work-life balance. It encourages empathy, respect for different lifestyles, and helps leaders and employees navigate cultural differences effectively. Inclusivity training ensures that organizational policies and practices are equitable and inclusive of all employees (Schein, 2010).

3. Comprehensive Employee Well-being Initiatives: Implementing holistic employee well-being initiatives that encompass physical, mental, and emotional health can significantly impact work-life balance. These initiatives may include fitness programs, stress management workshops, mindfulness training, and financial wellness seminars. By addressing various aspects of well-being, organizations support employees in achieving balance and resilience (Goetzel et al., 2002).

4. Flexible Work Arrangements: Offering flexible work arrangements, such as telecommuting, flexible hours, compressed workweeks, and job-sharing opportunities, allows employees to manage work commitments alongside personal responsibilities effectively. Flexible arrangements accommodate diverse needs and preferences, enhancing job satisfaction and productivity (Golden, 2001).

5. Promoting Boundaries and Time Management: Encouraging employees, including workaholic bosses, to set boundaries between work and personal life is essential. Policies that discourage after-hours emails, promote regular breaks, and emphasize the importance of taking vacations contribute to a healthier work-life balance. Time management training equips employees with skills to prioritize tasks, manage workload effectively, and avoid burnout (Covey, 1989).

Case Studies and Best Practices

Examining case studies of organizations that have successfully fostered a supportive organizational culture can provide valuable insights into effective strategies and best practices.

Google's Approach to Work-Life Integration: Google is renowned for its approach to work-life integration, emphasizing flexibility, autonomy, and trust. The company offers comprehensive wellness programs, mindfulness training, and resources for stress management. Google's commitment to employee well-being has contributed to high levels of job satisfaction, innovation, and retention (Schmidt & Rosenberg, 2014).

Microsoft's Focus on Well-being and Inclusion: Microsoft prioritizes employee well-being and inclusion through initiatives that promote work-life balance. These initiatives include flexible work options, mental health support, and diversity training. Microsoft's inclusive culture fosters a sense of belonging and supports employees in balancing professional and personal commitments (Microsoft, 2020).

Accenture's Diversity and Flexibility Initiatives: Accenture has implemented diversity and flexibility initiatives that support work-life balance for employees globally. These initiatives include flexible work arrangements, parental leave policies, and career development programs. Accenture's commitment to diversity and flexibility enhances employee engagement, productivity, and organizational resilience (Accenture, 2021).

Salesforce's Mental Health Awareness Campaigns: Salesforce has launched mental health awareness campaigns that promote open dialogue and reduce stigma around mental health issues. These campaigns include training for managers, access to counseling services, and resources for stress management. Salesforce's focus on mental health supports a supportive culture where employees feel valued and supported (Salesforce, 2021).

Fostering a supportive organizational culture that promotes work-life balance is essential for the well-being of employees, including workaholic bosses. By implementing strategies such as leadership development programs, cultural sensitivity training, and comprehensive well-being initiatives, organizations can create environments where employees thrive personally and professionally.

In the next sections, we will delve deeper into specific case studies, explore further best practices, and discuss practical recommendations for organizations to foster a supportive organizational culture conducive to work-life balance.

Chapter 6: Strategies for Achieving Work-Life Balance

Achieving work-life balance is a dynamic process that involves consciously managing responsibilities, setting boundaries, and prioritizing personal well-being alongside professional success. This chapter explores practical strategies and interventions for individuals, including workaholic bosses, to navigate the complexities of modern work environments while maintaining a fulfilling personal life.

Understanding Work-Life Balance

Work-life balance refers to the equilibrium individuals seek between their professional commitments and personal life responsibilities (Greenhaus & Allen, 2011). It involves managing time, energy, and attention effectively to prevent burnout, enhance overall well-being, and improve quality of life (Clark, 2000).

Challenges Faced by Workaholic Bosses: Workaholic bosses often struggle with work-life balance due to their intense dedication to work, tendency to prioritize professional responsibilities over personal needs, and difficulty disconnecting from work-related activities (Porter & Steers, 1973). These challenges can lead to increased stress, health issues, and strained relationships both at home and in the workplace.

Strategies for Work-Life Balance

Implementing effective strategies to achieve work-life balance requires a proactive approach that addresses individual behaviors, habits, and mindset. The following strategies are designed to help individuals, including workaholic bosses, foster balance and well-being in their professional and personal lives:

1. Time Management and Prioritization: Effective time management is crucial for balancing work and personal commitments. Techniques such as prioritizing tasks, setting realistic goals, and creating daily or weekly schedules can help individuals allocate time efficiently and reduce feelings of overwhelm (Allen, 2001).

2. Establishing Boundaries: Setting boundaries between work and personal life is essential for maintaining balance. This includes defining specific work hours, avoiding work-related activities during personal time, and learning to say no to excessive work demands (Eby et al., 2005).

3. Practicing Mindfulness and Stress Management: Mindfulness techniques, such as meditation and deep breathing exercises, can help individuals manage stress, improve focus, and enhance overall well-being (Kabat-Zinn, 1990). Incorporating regular breaks, physical exercise, and relaxation techniques into daily routines also supports stress management and mental health (Sonnentag & Fritz, 2007).

4. Utilizing Technology Wisely: While technology enables flexibility and connectivity, it can also blur the boundaries between work and personal life. Individuals should establish guidelines for technology use, such as turning off work notifications during non-work hours and creating digital-free zones at home (Derks et al., 2014).

5. Investing in Personal Development: Engaging in hobbies, pursuing interests outside of work, and investing in personal development activities, such as learning new skills or hobbies, promotes a well-rounded lifestyle and enhances overall life satisfaction (Deci & Ryan, 2000).

6. Seeking Social Support: Maintaining strong social connections and seeking support from friends, family, and colleagues can buffer the negative effects of work-related stress and foster emotional well-being (Thoits, 2011). Building a support network provides opportunities for relaxation, recreation, and meaningful connections outside of work.

Personal Effectiveness and Well-being

Achieving work-life balance is not only about managing time and tasks but also about nurturing personal effectiveness and well-being. Individuals, including workaholic bosses, can enhance their effectiveness and well-being by adopting holistic approaches that integrate professional success with personal fulfillment.

Case Study: Personal Effectiveness in Action *John, a senior manager at a consulting firm, struggled with workaholism and its impact on his personal life. By implementing structured time management techniques, establishing clear boundaries, and prioritizing regular exercise and family time, John successfully achieved a healthier work-life balance. His improved well-being translated into higher job satisfaction and enhanced relationships both at work and at home.*

Achieving and maintaining work-life balance is a continuous journey that requires self-awareness, intentional actions, and ongoing adjustments. By implementing strategies such as time management, boundary-setting, mindfulness practices, and personal development, individuals, including workaholic bosses, can navigate the complexities of work-life integration effectively.

In the next sections, we will explore case studies, best practices, and practical recommendations to support individuals in cultivating sustainable work-life balance and enhancing overall well-being.

Conclusion: Cultivating Balance and Well-being in a Workaholic World

Embracing Work-Life Balance as a Strategic Imperative

Throughout this book, we have embarked on a journey to understand the intricate dynamics of workaholic behavior, its impact on individuals and organizations, and effective strategies to foster a healthier, more balanced approach to work and life. In a world where workaholism is often glorified as a badge of honor, it becomes imperative to redefine success not just in terms of professional achievements but also in terms of holistic well-being and sustainable productivity.

Understanding Workaholism and Its Consequences: Workaholism, characterized by an obsessive drive to work excessively and compulsively, can lead to detrimental effects on both personal health and organizational dynamics. Workaholic bosses, driven by an insatiable need for achievement and perfectionism, often neglect their own well-being and inadvertently create environments where overwork is normalized (Robinson, 1998). This can result in increased stress, burnout, diminished creativity, and strained interpersonal relationships (Porter & Steers, 1973).

The Role of Organizational Culture: Organizational culture plays a pivotal role in shaping workaholic behaviors and attitudes towards work-life balance. Cultures that prioritize long hours, constant availability, and equate busyness with productivity can perpetuate workaholism (Schaufeli et al., 2009). Conversely, fostering a supportive culture that values work-life balance through clear policies, leadership support, and well-being initiatives is essential for mitigating the negative effects of workaholism and promoting employee engagement and satisfaction (Golden, 2001).

Strategies for Achieving Work-Life Balance

Individual Strategies: For individuals, including workaholic bosses, achieving work-life balance requires a proactive approach that integrates effective time management, boundary-setting, and prioritization of personal well-being. Strategies such as mindfulness practices, regular exercise, and cultivating hobbies outside of work not only enhance productivity but also foster resilience and overall life satisfaction (Kabat-Zinn, 1990).

Organizational Strategies: At the organizational level, implementing comprehensive policies and practices that support work-life balance is crucial. This includes offering flexible work arrangements, promoting inclusive leadership, and providing resources for mental health and wellness (Allen, 2001). Organizations that prioritize employee well-being not only attract top talent but also cultivate a culture of trust, innovation, and sustainable growth (Clark, 2000).

Path Forward: Integrating Insights into Practice

As we look to the future, integrating the insights gained from this exploration into everyday practices becomes paramount. Workaholic bosses and organizational leaders alike must embrace a paradigm shift towards valuing quality over quantity, well-being over sheer productivity, and collaboration over individual heroics (Goleman, 1995). By fostering environments that support work-life balance, organizations not only enhance employee satisfaction and retention but also contribute to overall societal well-being and economic prosperity (Greenhaus & Allen, 2011).

Embracing Diversity and Inclusivity: Recognizing the diverse needs and preferences of employees is essential for creating inclusive work environments where all individuals, regardless of their work style or personal circumstances, can thrive. Flexible policies that accommodate caregiving responsibilities, remote work options, and opportunities for professional development contribute to a culture of equity and respect (Eby et al., 2005).

Continuous Learning and Adaptation: Achieving and maintaining work-life balance is a journey that requires ongoing learning, adaptation, and a commitment to continuous improvement. Leaders must remain agile in responding to changing work dynamics, technological advancements, and societal shifts that impact work-life integration (Derks et al., 2014).

A Call to Action

In conclusion, cultivating balance and well-being in a workaholic world demands collective action and a shared commitment to human-centric values. By prioritizing work-life balance, embracing inclusive practices, and fostering environments that nurture both professional success and personal fulfillment, we pave the way for a future where individuals thrive, organizations flourish, and society benefits as a whole (Sonnentag & Fritz, 2007).

Let us embark on this journey together, bridging the gap between ambition and well-being, and shaping workplaces where workaholic bosses can lead with empathy, employees can thrive with resilience, and success is measured not just by what we achieve, but by how we live.

References

Chapter 1

Burke, R. J., & Matthiesen, S. B. (2004). Workaholism among Norwegian managers: Work and well-being outcomes. *Journal of Organizational Change Management, 17*(5), 459-470. https://doi.org/10.1108/09534810410554489

Maslach, C., Schaufeli, W. B., & Leiter, M. P. (2001). Job burnout. *Annual Review of Psychology, 52*(1), 397-422. https://doi.org/10.1146/annurev.psych.52.1.397

Ng, T. W. H., Sorensen, K. L., & Feldman, D. C. (2007). Dimensions, antecedents, and consequences of workaholism: A conceptual integration and extension. *Journal of Organizational Behavior, 28*(1), 111-136. https://doi.org/10.1002/job.424

Porter, G. (2001). Workaholic tendencies and the high potential for stress among co-workers. *International Journal of Stress Management, 8*(3), 147-164. https://doi.org/10.1023/A:1011341818792

Robinson, B. E. (2000). Workaholism: Bridging the gap between workplace, socio-cultural and family research. *Journal of Employment Counseling, 37*(1), 31-47. https://doi.org/10.1002/j.2161-1920.2000.tb01024.x

Stoeber, J., & Damian, L. E. (2016). Perfectionism in employees: Work engagement, workaholism, and burnout. *The Industrial-Organizational Psychologist, 54*(2), 75-84.

Taris, T. W., Schaufeli, W. B., & Verhoeven, L. C. (2005). Workaholism in the Netherlands: Measurement and implications for job strain and work-nonwork conflict. *Applied Psychology, 54*(1), 37-60. https://doi.org/10.1111/j.1464-0597.2005.00195.x

Chapter 2

American Psychiatric Association. (2013). *Diagnostic and statistical manual of mental disorders* (5th ed.). Arlington, VA: American Psychiatric Publishing.

Aron, A., Norman, C. C., Aron, E. N., & Lewandowski, G. W. (2002). Shared activities and marital satisfaction: Causal direction and self-expansion versus boredom. *Journal of Social and Personal Relationships, 19*(6), 835-852.

Burke, R. J., & Matthiesen, S. B. (2004). Workaholism among Norwegian managers: Work and well-being outcomes. *Journal of Organizational Change Management, 17*(5), 459-470.

Charnetski, C. J., & Brennan, F. X. (2001). The effect of stress on sexual arousal in men and women. *Journal of Human Stress, 7*(2), 5-13.

Goleman, D. (1995). *Emotional intelligence: Why it can matter more than IQ*. New York, NY: Bantam Books.

Gottman, J. M., & Silver, N. (1999). *The seven principles for making marriage work*. New York, NY: Three Rivers Press.

Hülsheger, U. R., Alberts, H. J. E. M., Feinholdt, A., & Lang, J. W. B. (2014). Benefits of mindfulness at work: The role of mindfulness in emotion regulation, emotional exhaustion, and job satisfaction. *Journal of Applied Psychology, 98*(2), 310-325.

Kabat-Zinn, J. (1990). *Full catastrophe living: Using the wisdom of your body and mind to face stress, pain, and illness*. New York, NY: Delacorte.

Kivimäki, M., Jokela, M., Nyberg, S. T., Singh-Manoux, A., Fransson, E. I., Alfredsson, L., ... & Virtanen, M. (2015). Long working hours and risk of coronary heart disease and stroke: A systematic review and meta-analysis of published and unpublished data for 603,838 individuals. *The Lancet, 386*(10005), 1739-1746.

Kossek, E. E., Baltes, B. B., & Matthews, R. A. (2011). How work-family research can finally have an impact in practice. *Industrial and Organizational Psychology, 4*(3), 277-283.

Maslach, C., Schaufeli, W. B., & Leiter, M. P. (2001). Job burnout. *Annual Review of Psychology, 52*, 397-422.

Mayer, E. A. (2011). Gut feelings: The emerging biology of gut-brain communication. *Nature Reviews Neuroscience, 12*(8), 453-466.

Ng, T. W., Sorensen, K. L., & Feldman, D. C. (2007). Dimensions, antecedents, and consequences of workaholism: A conceptual integration and extension. *Journal of Organizational Behavior, 28*(1), 111-136.

Perlow, L. A. (1999). The time famine: Toward a sociology of work time. *Administrative Science Quarterly, 44*(1), 57-81.

Porter, G. (2001). Workaholic tendencies and the high potential for stress among co-workers. *International Journal of Stress Management, 8*(2), 147-164.

Richardson, K. M., & Rothstein, H. R. (2008). Effects of occupational stress management intervention programs: A meta-analysis. *Journal of Occupational Health Psychology, 13*(1), 69-93.

Robinson, B. E. (2000). A typology of workaholics with implications for counselors. *Journal of Counseling & Development, 78*(1), 71-80.

Rosen, R. C. (2000). Prevalence and risk factors of sexual dysfunction in men and women. *Current Psychiatry Reports, 2*(3), 189-195.

Sharpe, M., & Wilks, D. (2002). Fatigue. *BMJ, 325*(7362), 480-483.

Shimazu, A., Schaufeli, W. B., Kamiyama, K., & Kawakami, N. (2012). Workaholism in Japan: Measurement and health implications. *Industrial Health, 50*(6), 491-502.

Selye, H. (1976). *The stress of life*. New York, NY: McGraw-Hill.

Stoeber, J., & Damian, L. E. (2016). Perfectionism in employees: Work engagement, workaholism, and burnout. *International Journal of Stress Management, 23*(3), 249-269.

Taris, T. W., Schaufeli, W. B., & Verhoeven, L. C. (2005). Workaholism in the Netherlands: Measurement and implications for job strain and work-nonwork conflict. *Applied Psychology, 54*(1), 37-60.

Van der Hulst, M. (2003). Long workhours and health. *Scandinavian Journal of Work, Environment & Health, 29*(3), 171-188.

Walker, M. P. (2017). *Why we sleep: Unlocking the power of sleep and dreams*. New York, NY: Scribner.

WHO & ILO. (2021). Long working hours and the risk of cardiovascular disease. *World Health Organization*.

Chapter 3

Aldana, S. G., & Pronk, N. P. (2001). Health promotion programs, modifiable health risks, and employee absenteeism. *Journal of Occupational and Environmental Medicine, 43*(1), 36-46.

Amabile, T. M., Conti, R., Coon, H., Lazenby, J., & Herron, M. (1996). Assessing the work environment for creativity. *Academy of Management Journal, 39*(5), 1154-1184.

Ashford, S. J., Lee, C., & Bobko, P. (1989). Content, causes, and consequences of job insecurity: A theory-based measure and substantive test. *Academy of Management Journal, 32*(4), 803-829.

Bakker, A. B., Demerouti, E., & Schaufeli, W. B. (2005). The crossover of burnout and work engagement among working couples. *Human Relations, 58*(5), 661-689.

Boswell, W. R., & Olson-Buchanan, J. B. (2007). The use of communication technologies after hours: The role of work attitudes and work-life conflict. *Journal of Management, 33*(4), 592-610.

Deloitte. (2020). *Mental health in the workplace*. Retrieved from Deloitte website.

Detert, J. R., & Burris, E. R. (2007). Leadership behavior and employee voice: Is the door really open? *Academy of Management Journal, 50*(4), 869-884.

Goetzel, R. Z., Ozminkowski, R. J., Sederer, L. I., & Mark, T. L. (2002). The business case for quality mental health services: Why employers should care about the mental health and well-being of their employees. *Journal of Occupational and Environmental Medicine, 44*(4), 320-330.

Goleman, D. (1995). *Emotional intelligence: Why it can matter more than IQ*. New York, NY: Bantam Books.

Hackman, J. R., & Oldham, G. R. (1976). Motivation through the design of work: Test of a theory. *Organizational Behavior and Human Performance, 16*(2), 250-279.

Hobfoll, S. E. (1989). Conservation of resources: A new attempt at conceptualizing stress. *American Psychologist, 44*(3), 513-524.

Huselid, M. A. (1995). The impact of human resource management practices on turnover, productivity, and corporate financial performance. *Academy of Management Journal, 38*(3), 635-672.

Judge, T. A., Bono, J. E., Thoresen, C. J., & Patton, G. K. (2001). The job satisfaction–job performance relationship: A qualitative and quantitative review. *Psychological Bulletin, 127*(3), 376-407.

Karasek, R. A. (1979). Job demands, job decision latitude, and mental strain: Implications for job redesign. *Administrative Science Quarterly, 24*(2), 285-308.

Katz, D., & Kahn, R. L. (1978). *The social psychology of organizations* (2nd ed.). New York, NY: Wiley.

Kossek, E. E., Baltes, B. B., & Matthews, R. A. (2011). How work-family research can finally have an impact in practice. *Industrial and Organizational Psychology, 4*(3), 277-283.

Maslach, C., & Jackson, S. E. (1981). The measurement of experienced burnout. *Journal of Occupational Behavior, 2*(2), 99-113.

Melchior, M., Caspi, A., Milne, B. J., Danese, A., Poulton, R., & Moffitt, T. E. (2007). Work stress precipitates depression and anxiety in young, working women and men. *Psychological Medicine, 37*(8), 1119-1129.

Meyer, J. P., & Allen, N. J. (1991). A three-component conceptualization of organizational commitment. *Human Resource Management Review, 1*(1), 61-89.

Porter, G. (2001). Workaholic tendencies and the high potential for stress among co-workers. *International Journal of Stress Management, 8*(2), 147-164.

Rhoades, L., & Eisenberger, R. (2002). Perceived organizational support: A review of the literature. *Journal of Applied Psychology, 87*(4), 698-714.

Richardson, K. M., & Rothstein, H. R. (2008). Effects of occupational stress management intervention programs: A meta-analysis. *Journal of Occupational Health Psychology, 13*(1), 69-93.

Salesforce. (2021). *Wellness at Salesforce*. Retrieved from Salesforce website.

Sapolsky, R. M. (2004). *Why zebras don't get ulcers: The acclaimed guide to stress, stress-related diseases, and coping* (3rd ed.). New York, NY: Holt Paperbacks.

Schein, E. H. (2010). *Organizational culture and leadership* (4th ed.). San Francisco, CA: Jossey-Bass.

Schmidt, E., & Rosenberg, J. (2014). *How Google works*. New York, NY: Grand Central Publishing.

Unilever. (2019). *Employee well-being at Unilever*.

Chapter 4

Adobe. (2018). *Work-life balance at Adobe*. Retrieved from Adobe website.

Allen, D. (2001). *Getting things done: The art of stress-free productivity*. New York, NY: Penguin Books.

American Express. (2017). *American Express wellness programs*. Retrieved from American Express website.

Beck, J. S. (2011). *Cognitive behavior therapy: Basics and beyond* (2nd ed.). New York, NY: Guilford Press.

Covey, S. R. (1989). *The 7 habits of highly effective people: Powerful lessons in personal change*. New York, NY: Free Press.

Deci, E. L., & Ryan, R. M. (1987). The support of autonomy and the control of behavior. *Journal of Personality and Social Psychology, 53*(6), 1024-1037.

Detert, J. R., & Burris, E. R. (2007). Leadership behavior and employee voice: Is the door really open? *Academy of Management Journal, 50*(4), 869-884.

EY. (2019). *Flexible work policy at Ernst & Young*. Retrieved from EY website.

Fritz, C., & Sonnentag, S. (2006). Recovery, health, and job performance: Effects of weekend experiences. *Journal of Occupational Health Psychology, 11*(3), 187-199.

Goetzel, R. Z., Ozminkowski, R. J., Sederer, L. I., & Mark, T. L. (2002). The business case for quality mental health services: Why employers should care about the mental health and well-being of their employees. *Journal of Occupational and Environmental Medicine, 44*(4), 320-330.

Golden, T. D. (2001). Telecommuting and the quality of life: A review of the literature and implications for the future. *Journal of Business and Psychology, 15*(3), 317-329.

Hackman, J. R., & Oldham, G. R. (1976). Motivation through the design of work: Test of a theory. *Organizational Behavior and Human Performance, 16*(2), 250-279.

Kabat-Zinn, J. (1994). *Wherever you go, there you are: Mindfulness meditation in everyday life*. New York, NY: Hyperion.

Kossek, E. E., Baltes, B. B., & Matthews, R. A. (2011). How work-family research can finally have an impact in practice. *Industrial and Organizational Psychology, 4*(3), 277-283.

Microsoft. (2020). *Employee well-being at Microsoft*.

Oates, W. E. (1971). *Confessions of a workaholic: The facts about work addiction*. New York, NY: World Publishing Company.

Richardson, K. M., & Rothstein, H. R. (2008). Effects of occupational stress management intervention programs: A meta-analysis. *Journal of Occupational Health Psychology, 13*(1), 69-93.

Schein, E. H. (2010). *Organizational culture and leadership* (4th ed.). San Francisco, CA: Jossey-Bass.

Siegrist, J. (1996). Adverse health effects of high-effort/low-reward conditions. *Journal of Occupational Health Psychology, 1*(1), 27-41.

Spence, J. T., & Robbins, A. S. (1992). Workaholism: Definition, measurement, and preliminary results. *Journal of Personality Assessment, 58*(1), 160-178.

Stoeber, J., & Damian, L. E. (2016). Perfectionism in employees: Work engagement, workaholism, and burnout. *The Psychological Record, 66*(4), 545-562.

Chapter 5

Accenture. (2021). *Diversity and inclusion at Accenture*. Retrieved from Accenture website.

Covey, S. R. (1989). *The 7 habits of highly effective people: Powerful lessons in personal change*. New York, NY: Free Press.

Deci, E. L., & Ryan, R. M. (1987). The support of autonomy and the control of behavior. *Journal of Personality and Social Psychology, 53*(6), 1024-1037.

Detert, J. R., & Burris, E. R. (2007). Leadership behavior and employee voice: Is the door really open? *Academy of Management Journal, 50*(4), 869-884.

Fritz, C., & Sonnentag, S. (2006). Recovery, health, and job performance: Effects of weekend experiences. *Journal of Occupational Health Psychology, 11*(3), 187-199.

Goleman, D. (1995). *Emotional intelligence: Why it can matter more than IQ*. New York, NY: Bantam Books.

Goetzel, R. Z., Ozminkowski, R. J., Sederer, L. I., & Mark, T. L. (2002). The business case for quality mental health services: Why employers should care about the mental health and well-being of their employees. *Journal of Occupational and Environmental Medicine, 44*(4), 320-330.

Golden, T. D. (2001). Telecommuting and the quality of life: A review of the literature and implications for the future. *Journal of Business and Psychology, 15*(3), 317-329.

Johnson & Johnson. (2018). *Employee wellness programs at Johnson & Johnson*. Retrieved from Johnson & Johnson website.

Kossek, E. E., Baltes, B. B., & Matthews, R. A. (2011). How work-family research can finally have an impact in practice. *Industrial and Organizational Psychology, 4*(3), 277-283.

Microsoft. (2020). *Employee well-being at Microsoft*. Retrieved from Microsoft website.

Patagonia. (2020). *Family-friendly policies at Patagonia*. Retrieved from Patagonia website.

PricewaterhouseCoopers (PwC). (2021). *Flexibility and well-being programs at PwC*. Retrieved from PwC website.

Salesforce. (2021). *Mental health initiatives at Salesforce*. Retrieved from Salesforce website.

Schein, E. H. (2010). *Organizational culture and leadership* (4th ed.). San Francisco, CA: Jossey-Bass.

Schmidt, E., & Rosenberg, J. (2014). *How Google works*. New York, NY: Grand Central Publishing.

Chapter 6

Allen, T. D. (2001). Family-supportive work environments: The role of organizational perceptions. *Journal of Vocational Behavior, 58*(3), 414-435.

Clark, S. C. (2000). Work/family border theory: A new theory of work/family balance. *Human Relations, 53*(6), 747-770.

Deci, E. L., & Ryan, R. M. (2000). The "what" and "why" of goal pursuits: Human needs and the self-determination of behavior. *Psychological Inquiry, 11*(4), 227-268.

Derks, D., Bakker, A. B., Peters, P., & van Wingerden, P. (2014). Work-related smartphone use, work-family conflict and family role performance: The role of segmentation preference. *Human Relations, 67*(6), 738-761.

Eby, L. T., Casper, W. J., Lockwood, A., Bordeaux, C., & Brinley, A. (2005). Work and family research in IO/OB: Content analysis and review of the literature (1980–2002). *Journal of Vocational Behavior, 66*(1), 124-197.

Greenhaus, J. H., & Allen, T. D. (2011). Work-family balance: A review and extension of the literature. In J. C. Quick & L. E. Tetrick (Eds.), *Handbook of occupational health psychology* (2nd ed., pp. 165-183). Washington, DC: American Psychological Association.

Kabat-Zinn, J. (1990). *Full catastrophe living: Using the wisdom of your body and mind to face stress, pain, and illness*. New York, NY: Delacorte Press.

Porter, L. W., & Steers, R. M. (1973). Organizational, work, and personal factors in employee turnover and absenteeism. *Psychological Bulletin, 80*(2), 151-176.

Sonnentag, S., & Fritz, C. (2007). The recovery experience questionnaire: Development and validation of a measure for assessing recuperation and unwinding from work. *Journal of Occupational Health Psychology, 12*(3), 204-221.

Thoits, P. A. (2011). Mechanisms linking social ties and support to physical and mental health. *Journal of Health and Social Behavior, 52*(2), 145-161.

Conclusions

Allen, T. D. (2001). Family-supportive work environments: The role of organizational perceptions. *Journal of Vocational Behavior, 58*(3), 414-435.

Clark, S. C. (2000). Work/family border theory: A new theory of work/family balance. *Human Relations, 53*(6), 747-770.

Derks, D., Bakker, A. B., Peters, P., & van Wingerden, P. (2014). Work-related smartphone use, work-family conflict and family role performance: The role of segmentation preference. *Human Relations, 67*(6), 738-761.

Eby, L. T., Casper, W. J., Lockwood, A., Bordeaux, C., & Brinley, A. (2005). Work and family research in IO/OB: Content analysis and review of the literature (1980–2002). *Journal of Vocational Behavior, 66*(1), 124-197.

Goleman, D. (1995). *Emotional intelligence: Why it can matter more than IQ*. New York, NY: Bantam Books.

Golden, T. D. (2001). Telecommuting and the quality of life: A review of the literature and implications for the future. *Journal of Business and Psychology, 15*(3), 317-329.

Greenhaus, J. H., & Allen, T. D. (2011). Work-family balance: A review and extension of the literature. In J. C. Quick & L. E. Tetrick (Eds.), *Handbook of occupational health psychology* (2nd ed., pp. 165-183). Washington, DC: American Psychological Association.

Kabat-Zinn, J. (1990). *Full catastrophe living: Using the wisdom of your body and mind to face stress, pain, and illness*. New York, NY: Delacorte Press.

Porter, L. W., & Steers, R. M. (1973). Organizational, work, and personal factors in employee turnover and absenteeism. *Psychological Bulletin, 80*(2), 151-176.

Robinson, B. E. (1998). The micromanager: Diagnosis and cure. *Journal of Business Strategy, 19*(3), 21-24.

Schaufeli, W. B., Taris, T. W., & Bakker, A. B. (2009). It takes two to tango: Workaholism is working excessively and working compulsively. In S. L. Albrecht (Ed.), *Handbook of employee engagement: Perspectives, issues, research and practice* (pp. 855-873). Cheltenham, UK: Edward Elgar Publishing.

Sonnentag, S., & Fritz, C. (2007). The recovery experience questionnaire: Development and validation of a measure for assessing recuperation and unwinding from work. *Journal of Occupational Health Psychology, 12*(3), 204-221.

These references provide foundational knowledge and support for the conclusions drawn in the book regarding work-life balance, workaholism, organizational culture, and strategies for fostering well-being in the workplace

Raul Dominguez is a highly experienced practitioner and researcher in the field of Industrial-Organizational Psychology. He brings a wealth of knowledge and expertise to the subject, helping individuals and organizations improve workplace effectiveness and employee well-being.

His expertise in IO Psychology shines through, making "Workaholic Bosses: Impact on Health and the Workplace" an essential resource for anyone looking to improve workplace effectiveness and employee well-being.

www.ingramcontent.com/pod-product-compliance
Lightning Source LLC
Chambersburg PA
CBHW071842210526
45479CB00001B/256